D1462059

Elephants

Michael and Jane Pelusey

Marshall Cavendish
Benchmark
New York

This edition first published in 2009 in the United States of America by Marshall Cavendish Benchmark.

Marshall Cavendish Benchmark
99 White Plains Road
Tarrytown, NY 10591
www.marshallcavendish.us

First published in 2008 by
MACMILLAN EDUCATION AUSTRALIA PTY LTD
15–19 Claremont Street, South Yarra 3141

Visit our Web site at www.macmillan.com.au or go directly to www.macmillanlibrary.com.au

Associated companies and representatives throughout the world.

Library of Congress Cataloging-in-Publication Data

Pelusey, Michael.
    Elephants / by Michael and Jane Pelusey.
    p. cm. — (Zoo animals)
    Includes index.
    ISBN 978-0-7614-3148-0
    1. Elephants—Juvenile literature. 2. Zoo animals—Juvenile literature.
    I. Pelusey, Jane. II. Title.
    SF408.6.E44P45 2008
    636.967—dc22

                                                      2008001665

Edited by Margaret Maher
Text and cover design by Christine Deering
Page layout by Christine Deering
Illustrations by Gaston Vanzet

Printed in the United States

Acknowledgments
Michael and Jane Pelusey would like to thank Perth Zoo, Melbourne Zoo, Werribee Wildlife Zoo, and Taronga Zoo for their assistance with this project.

Cover photograph: Asian elephants in zoo enclosure, courtesy of Pelusey Photography.

All photographs © Pelusey Photography except for Global Gypsies, **3**, **6**, **11**, **18**; Perth Zoo, **7**, **30**; Taronga Zoo, **13**.

1 3 5 6 4 2

Contents

Glossary words

When a word is printed in **bold**, you can look up its meaning in the Glossary on page 31.

Zoos

Zoos are places where animals that are usually **wild** are kept in **enclosures**. Some zoos have a lot of space for animals to move about. They are called wildlife zoos.

A wildlife zoo has a lot of space for large animals to roam.

Zoo Animals

Zoos keep all kinds of animals. People go to zoos to learn about animals. Some animals may become **extinct** if left to live in the wild.

People watch an elephant swimming at a zoo.

Elephants

Elephants are very big animals with large ears and long **trunks**. There are three kinds of elephants. The African bush elephant and African forest elephant have big ears and straight backs.

big ears

long trunk

The African bush elephant is the biggest land animal in the world.

Asian elephants have smaller ears and a sloping back. They are much smaller than African elephants.

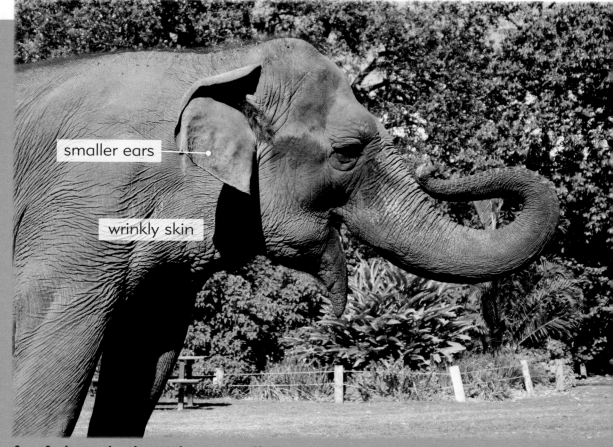

smaller ears

wrinkly skin

An Asian elephant has small ears and wrinkly skin.

In the Wild

In the wild, African bush elephants live mainly in the drier areas of Africa. African forest elephants live in **rain forests**.

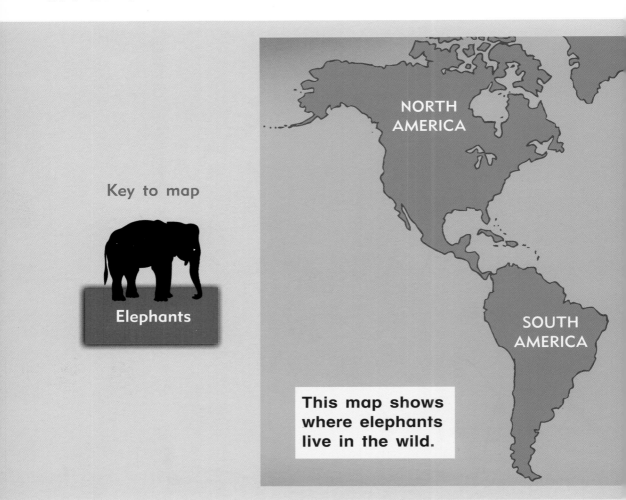

Key to map

Elephants

NORTH AMERICA

SOUTH AMERICA

This map shows where elephants live in the wild.

Asian elephants live in rain forest areas of southern Asia. All elephants live in family groups.

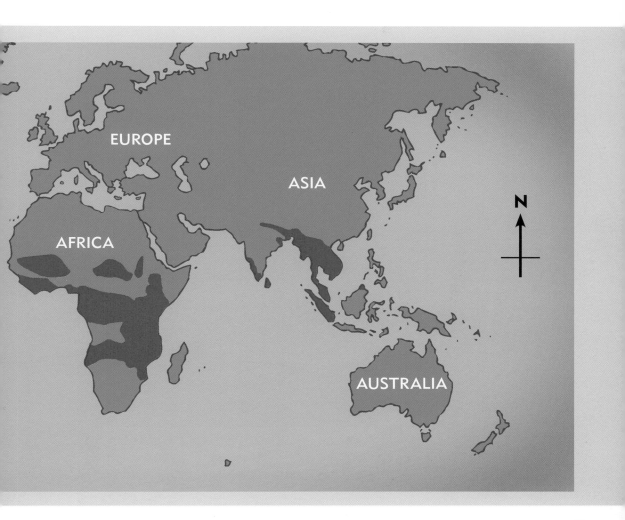

Threats to Survival

The biggest threat to survival for elephants is forest clearing. Humans cut down trees for timber and use the land for farming.

Asian elephants lived on this land before it was cleared.

Poachers, who shoot elephants for their **ivory** tusks, are also a threat to elephants' survival.

Elephants' ivory tusks are valuable to poachers.

Zoo Homes

In zoos, elephants live in large enclosures. These enclosures are often built so they are like the elephants' home in the wild.

fence to keep visitors out

sand to roll in

water to play in and to drink

This elephant enclosure has sand, water, and rocks, like the elephants' home in the wild.

Elephants have more space to roam at a wildlife zoo.

natural environment to roam around

grassy area

This large enclosure is the African elephant's home.

Zoo Food

Elephants need to eat different types of food to stay healthy. They eat eighty-eight pounds (40 kg) of food every day.

An elephant's zoo food
hay
fresh fruit
leaves
frozen fruit
popcorn
vegetarian **pellets**

A zookeeper delivers the hay for the elephants.

Feeding

Elephants are fed several times a day. The elephants use their trunks to pick up and put food in their mouths.

The elephants' main food is hay.

Zoo Health

Zookeepers look after the elephants so they stay healthy. Keepers train the elephants to lift their feet. This allows the keeper to check the feet for sores.

The keeper checks the elephant's feet once a week.

Every day, the keepers scrub the elephants and check their skin and teeth for diseases. They also take a blood sample to test for health problems.

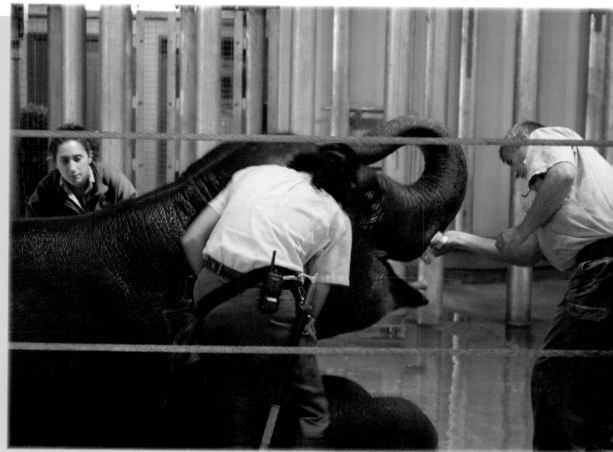

Zookeepers scrub the elephant's skin and teeth.

Baby Elephants

A mother elephant has one or two **calves** at a time. It takes twenty-two months for a calf to grow inside its mother.

An elephant calf can weigh up to 230 pounds (105 kg) at birth.

A baby elephant can stand up one hour after it is born. Young elephants stop feeding from their mothers when they are two years old.

As young elephants grow up, they learn to care for themselves.

How Zoos Are Saving Elephants

Zoos help save badly treated and **endangered** elephants. Elephants are very strong. Some are trained to carry logs or transport people. These elephants may be badly treated and need rescuing.

This elephant was trained to carry people.

Asian elephants are endangered in the wild. When forests are cleared, the elephants are left with little food. Zoos work with other organizations to raise money to save these elephants.

These three elephants were saved from a logging camp in Thailand.

Zoos often work together. Elephants are moved between different zoos to **breed** with other elephants. Some elephants are born in Asia and then moved to zoos around the world.

These elephants were moved from Thailand to Australia.

Elephants rescued from work camps are placed in zoos around the world. Some elephants are taught to paint pictures. These pictures can be sold to raise money to save more elephants.

This elephant has been taught how to paint pictures.

Meet Kirsty, an Elephant Keeper

Kirsty trains the elephant to flap its ears.

Question How did you become a zookeeper?

Answer I did work experience at zoos when I was at school. I then did a course at a community college.

Question How long have you been a keeper?

Answer I have been a keeper for seven years.

Kirsty checks the elephant's skin for rashes and scratches.

Question   What other animals have you worked with?

Answer   I have worked with a lot of animals, including otters, bears, and orangutans.

Question   What do you like about your job?

Answer   I love working with animals that learn to trust you.

A Day in the Life of a Zookeeper

Zookeepers have certain jobs to do each day. The elephants are big animals, so a team of zookeepers looks after them. The keepers do their tasks at different times each day.

8:00 a.m.

Let the elephants out of the night enclosure.

11:00 a.m.

Give the elephants toys to play with.

1:00 p.m.

Feed the elephants some hay.

3:00 p.m.

Take the elephants for a swim.

Zoos Around the World

There are many zoos around the world. The Taronga Park Zoo is located in Sydney, in Australia. The zoo has five Asian elephants. These elephants were rescued from work camps in Thailand.

The Taronga Park Zoo has a pool so the elephants can swim.

The Taronga Park Zoo keeps the four female elephants and one male elephant in an enclosure. The enclosure has a big swimming pool. The zoo hopes to breed these elephants.

The elephants have toys to play with in their enclosure.

The Importance of Zoos

Zoos do very important work. They:

- help people learn about animals
- save endangered animals and animals that are treated badly

Elephants can live safely in zoos.

Glossary

breed	keep animals so that they can produce babies
calves	baby elephants
enclosures	the fenced areas where animals are kept in zoos
endangered	at a high risk of becoming extinct
extinct	no longer living on Earth
ivory	the hard, white substance that elephant tusks are made of
pellets	small balls of dried food
plains	wide, flat grasslands with few trees
poachers	people who hunt animals illegally
rain forests	thick forests where the rainfall is high
trunks	elephants' long noses
wild	living in its natural environment and not taken care of by humans

Index